Gabriel Grape

Fruit of Kindness

Yira Bernard Jones

Edited by Katherine Ungerecht

Scripture quotations are taken from the Holy Bible, New Living Translation, copyright
©1996, 2004, 2007, 2013, 2015 by Tyndale House Foundation. Used by permission of
Tyndale House Publishers, Inc., Carol Stream, Illinois 60188. All rights reserved.

WestBow Press books may be ordered through booksellers or by contacting:

WestBow Press
A Division of Thomas Nelson & Zondervan
1663 Liberty Drive
Bloomington, IN 47403
www.westbowpress.com
1 (866) 928-1240

ISBN: 978-1-9736-1634-4 (sc)
ISBN: 978-1-9736-1635-1 (e)

Library of Congress Control Number: 2018900196

Printed in China.

WestBow Press rev. date: 9/24/2018

WestBow
PRESS®
A DIVISION OF THOMAS NELSON
& ZONDERVAN

Gabriel Grape

"This book is a gift for"

_____

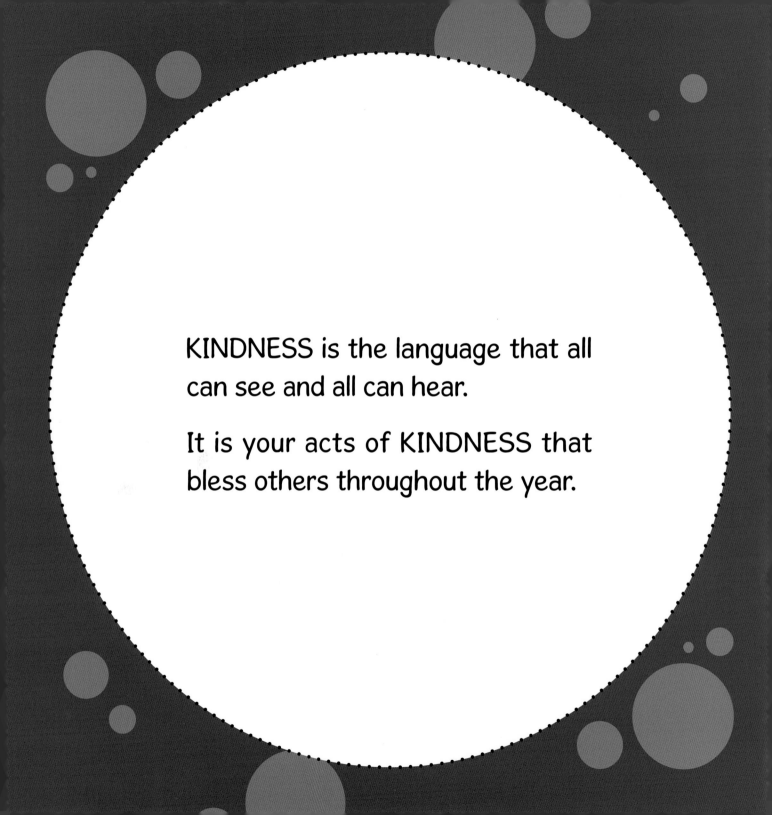

KINDNESS is the language that all can see and all can hear.

It is your acts of KINDNESS that bless others throughout the year.

KINDNESS is a special fruit that makes you very nice.

It is compassion, love, and selflessness for others at no price.

Ephesians 4:32 Instead, be kind to each other, tenderhearted, forgiving one another, just as God through Christ has forgiven you.

It makes you want to give when others simply take.

And it shows you how to love when others want to hate.

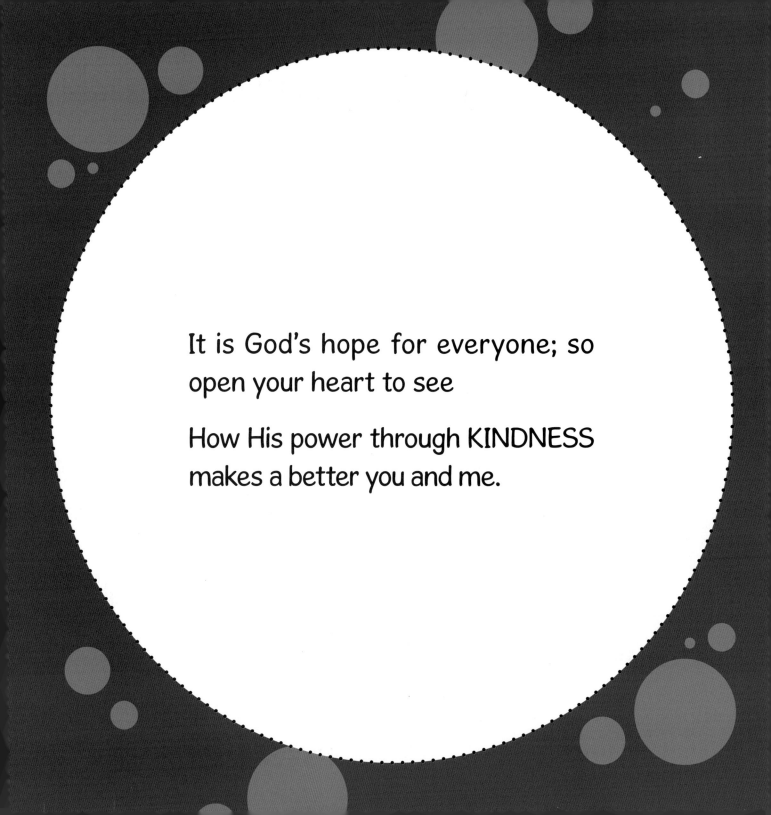

It is God's hope for everyone; so open your heart to see

How His power through KINDNESS makes a better you and me.

Ephesians 1:8 He has showered his kindness on us, along with all wisdom and understanding.

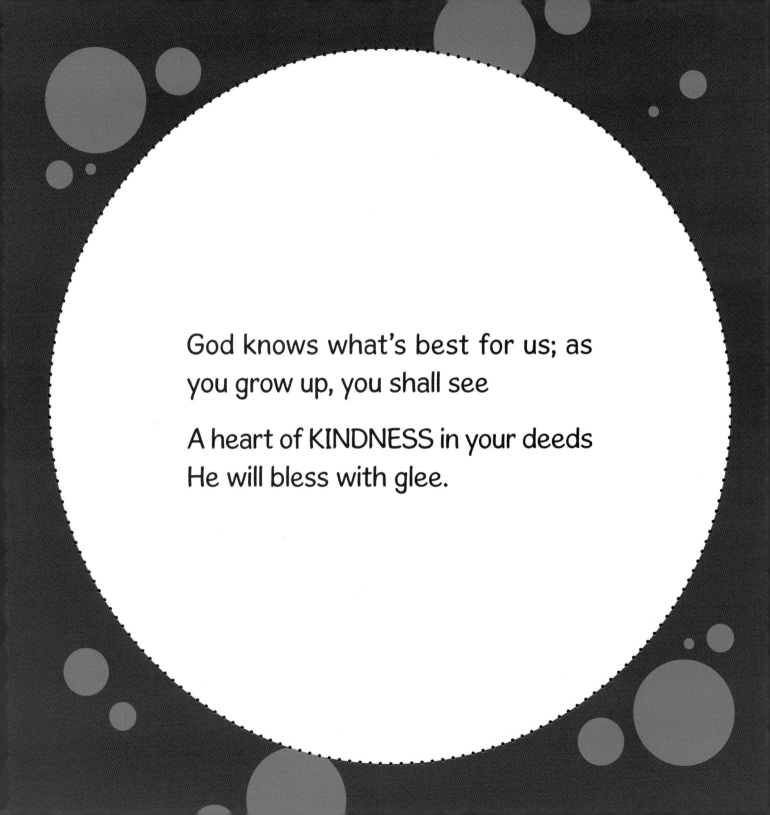

God knows what's best for us; as
you grow up, you shall see

A heart of KINDNESS in your deeds
He will bless with glee.

James 3:17 But the wisdom from above is first of all pure. It is also peace loving, gentle at all times, and willing to yield to others. It is full of mercy and the fruit of good deeds. It shows no favoritism and is always sincere.

He wants us to be nice and helpful to our friends—

To share and to be generous with love that never ends.

God also wants us to be humble and KIND toward all others...

That means strangers, even enemies, your sisters, and your brothers.

Luke 14:11 For those who exalt themselves will be humbled, and those who humble themselves will be exalted.

KINDNESS never made a man or woman grow upset.

In fact, it helps to bring a smile to someone in a fret.

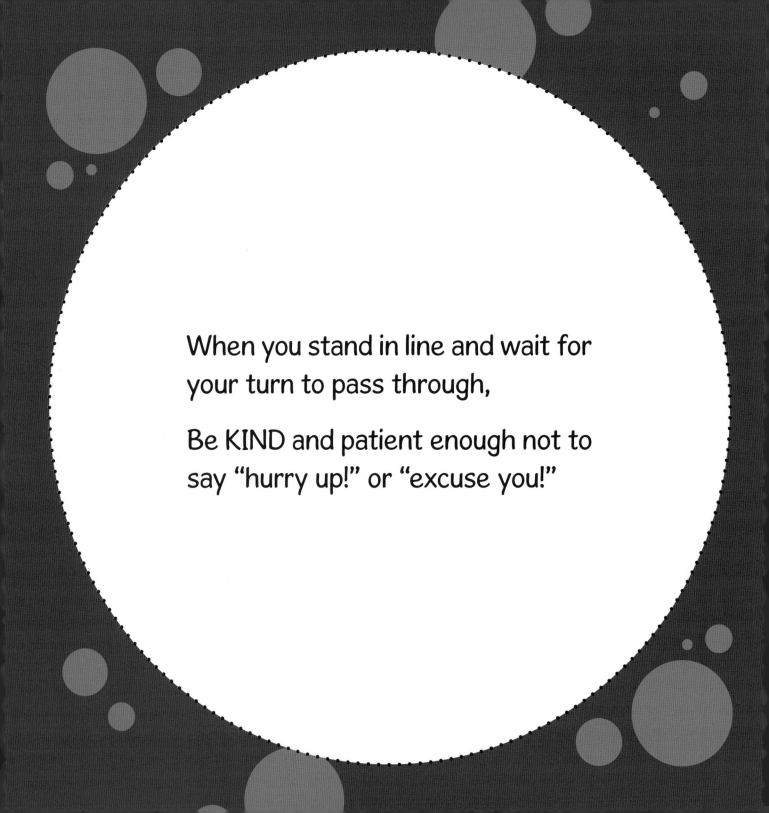

When you stand in line and wait for your turn to pass through,

Be KIND and patient enough not to say "hurry up!" or "excuse you!"

Romans 2:4 Don't you see how wonderfully kind, tolerant, and patient God is with you? Does this mean nothing to you? Can't you see that His kindness is intended to turn you from your sin?

If all of us were KIND and filled this world with care,

It would be a wonder to see love fill the air.

All would be happy to know they have a friend

In all who kindly touched their life now or at the end.

Can we have KINDNESS in our heart?
Is that so hard to ask?

To bless by smiling, helping, giving,
and not complaining at the task.

Romans 12:8 If your gift is to encourage others, be encouraging. If it is giving, give generously. If God has given you leadership ability, take the responsibility seriously. And if you have a gift for showing kindness to others, do it gladly.

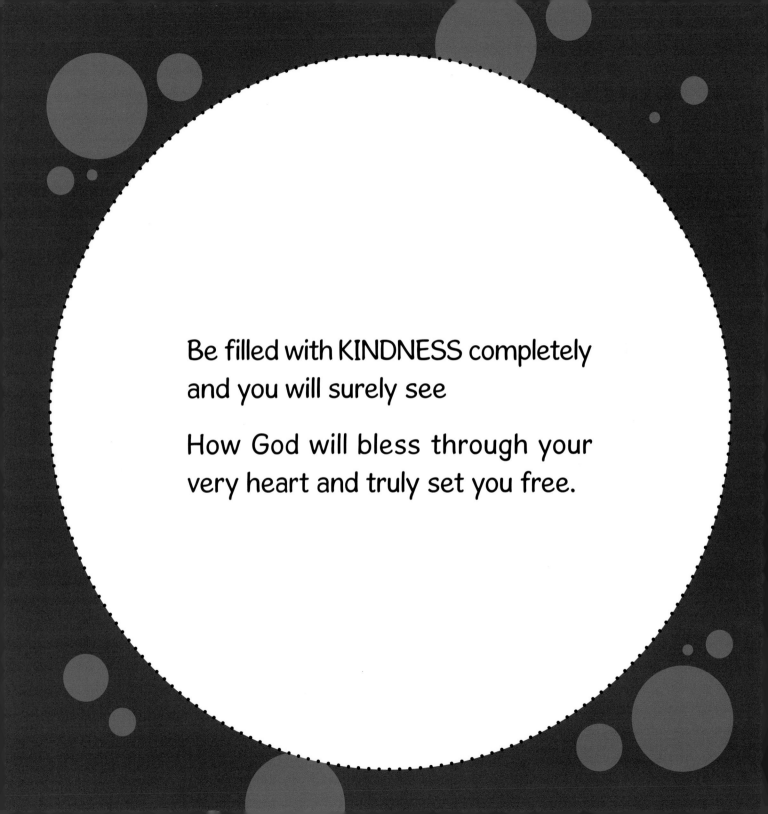

Be filled with KINDNESS completely
and you will surely see

How God will bless through your
very heart and truly set you free.

KINDNESS can change our world.

It starts with only ONE ACT of KINDNESS and spreads.

KINDNESS is free and it is powerful, so give it to everyone!

Be kind all the time and you will be filled with much joy and peace.

Child's Prayer:

Dear God, I pray that You fill me with the fruit of KINDNESS. Thank you for putting kindness on our hearts. Help me to be a blessing to all those around me by being kind and selfless. If someone is in need, use me to be kind and help them. Place on my heart what You would want me to do to be more like You. Help me to listen and obey. Jesus, come into my heart and move me to be kind always. Amen.

From the Author:

Do children understand how God wants our hearts to be filled with love, joy, peace, patience, kindness, goodness, faithfulness, gentleness, and self-control? Fruity Friends is a fun and engaging collection of books that teach children all about the Fruit of the Holy Spirit (Galatians 5:22-23). By using God's word in a fun way, each fruity character encourages the child to be like the character describes — loving, joyful, peaceful, patient, kind, good, faithful, gentle, and self-controlled. My hope is to show a glimpse of a mighty God who loves us greatly and gently shapes our character. Let us be more like Him today than we were yesterday and more like Him tomorrow than we are today.

In addition to revealing God's awesome love, the "Fruity Friends" collection will help to serve others, as a portion from the sale of these books will be given to a non-profit organization that cares for orphans and rescues children in need. To Him be the glory!

For more information, please visit us at **www.fruityfriendsbooks.com**